COLLECTING

SYLVAC

COLLECTING

SYLVAC

Mick and Derry Collins

THE SYLVAC COLLECTORS CIRCLE

CONTENTS

Forward   5

Sylvac Advertisements   6

Sylvac - Its History   8

The Sylvac Collectors Circle   10

Recognition   11

Sylvac 'Lookalikes'   16

Finishes   18

Rarity and Value   20

Locating Sylvac   21

Shaw & Copestake Pottery and Sylvac Ware   22

Index to Mould Numbers   69

Publications   71

Acknowledgements

Our thanks go to Jonathan, Kate and Bo Collins for their help (and tolerance!) in various ways, to Bob Irwin at J.A. Hewes (Photographers) and to Derrick Tyler at Selsey Press for his invaluable advice and help. Thanks also to Tableware International, International Trade Publications for their kind permission to use the trade advertisements.

4

FORWARD

The idea for creating this book came about as a result of the hundreds of SylvaC queries we've received over the ten years that we've run The SylvaC Collectors Circle and the continued requests for our very successful earlier publication, AN INTRODUCTION TO SYLVAC, now out of print. As many questions have come up time and time again we thought it would help collectors and would-be collectors if we could put down some of the answers in writing and combine them in a similar format to the earlier book. There are many misconceptions about SylvaC and we hope, through this book, to put some of them right. Everything about collecting should be enjoyable (apart from the empty pocket!) and collecting SylvaC is no exception. Very many people already have discovered the joys of this particular hobby and are amazed at the wide range of products that were produced by the creators of SylvaC - Shaw and Copestake Ltd. It is a tribute to the talents of their model-makers that the ideas they realised are now the objects of desire for hoards of collectors in this country and abroad. From ordinary household items, such as cups, saucers and plates to wonderfully crafted animals, in either caricature or life-like appearances, there is something to appeal to the budding SylvaC collector. Generally, it is a case of one piece and you're hooked! There are many things the new collector should look for when starting out and we very much hope that this book will play an important part in the learning process.

All of the pieces pictured in this book were photographed by us and are from our own collection, built up since the early 1980's, when we first became hooked!

Mick and Derry Collins, Horndean, Hampshire.

August 1998.

DEDICATION

This book is dedicated to Dad, Leonard Frank Collins, sadly no longer with us but from whom we inherited the collecting bug.

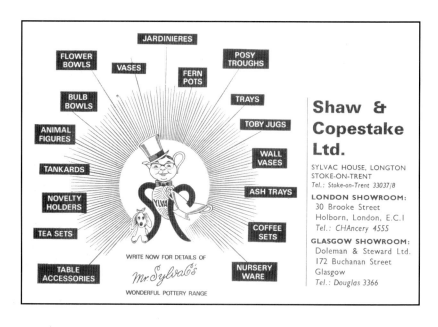

Shaw & Copestake Ltd.

SYLVAC HOUSE, LONGTON
STOKE-ON-TRENT
Tel.: Stoke-on-Trent 33037/8

LONDON SHOWROOM:
30 Brooke Street
Holborn, London, E.C.1
Tel.: CHAncery 4555

GLASGOW SHOWROOM:
Doleman & Steward Ltd.
172 Buchanan Street
Glasgow
Tel.: Douglas 3366

FLOWER BOWLS,
BASKETS,
JARDINIERES,
VASES,
BULB BOWLS,
JUGS,
& ANIMALS

Shaw and
Copestake Ltd.

Sylvan Works,
Longton,
Stoke-on-Trent,
England

1960's SylvaC Advertisements

6

SHAW & COPESTAKE LTD
LONGTON • STOKE - ON - TRENT • ENGLAND

1960's SylvaC Advertisement

7

Sylvac - Its History

The business of Shaw and Copestake, the manufacturers of Sylvac, was founded in 1894 in Longton, Stoke-on-Trent, Staffordshire and in the early years production consisted mainly of ornate vases, jugs, jardinieres, clock sets, etc. Towards the end of the 1920's they began to produce wares in a cellulose, or painted, finish and started to move away from their existing lines, realising that there was an emerging market for novelty wares and ornaments. In the early 1930's animals and figures in the cellulose finish were produced and these led to a whole range of items known as novelties and fancies - really fairground-type ware, found also in seaside gift shops and the like. As the market became more and more demanding, production was really geared up and a new type of coloured matt glazing was introduced. The well-known green Sylvac dogs and rabbits, found sitting on shelves, window sills and mantlepieces everywhere, were of this era. One of the company directors, Richard Hull Jnr., wanted a name for all of this type of ware and the name Sylvac was born, circa 1936, the name itself formed from the name of the then works or factory, the Sylvan Works. The pottery could not be called Sylvan Ware because there was already that name in existence, elsewhere, so the 'S' from Shaw and the 'C' from Copestake were used to work around Sylvan and so it became - Sylvac! Although there were hundreds of lines in production at that time, the new name was not used on the actual pottery moulds until some time later. Identification continued to be by label, affixed to the products, until, gradually, the change was introduced. Most Sylvac pieces actually made in the 1930's do not therefore have the name impressed into the base.

In the late 1930's there was an association with the company Thomas Lawrence (Longton) Ltd., who produced Falcon Ware and whose early lines were similar to those of Shaw and Copestake. The association, which came about because Richard Hull married the daughter of the Thomas Lawrence proprietor John Grundy, led to joint production of Sylvac and eventual absorption by Shaw and Copestake in the mid-1960's. Both companies operated a mould numbering system (the term 'system' is used very loosely!) of their pieces but the joint production and similar numbering has led, since, to a lot of confusion amongst Sylvac collectors.

Production of the coloured matt glaze items continued for many years, with many lines being withdrawn and new ones added as tastes changed, but in the late 1940's / early 1950's, a new finish, that is now referred to as the bright glaze finish (in other words, the shiny or gloss finish), was used. Some matt items, however, were still produced right up until the demise of the company in 1982, but it was the bright glaze finish that really took over for the majority of the company's products. Their lines continued to be popular throughout the fifties and sixties, with animals and novelties still the highest output but there were also vases, jugs, household items, flower pots, posy holders, bowls and troughs, etc., etc., all produced for the U.K. and export to Australia, Canada, New Zealand and South Africa. For a short while, even pottery brooches and earrings were manufactured! It has been said that, in the early 1950's, every house in the U.K. had at least one piece of SylvaC in it. Nevertheless, at the end of the 1970's business declined and, in 1982, Shaw and Copestake finished, leading to the factory being operated for a while as a workers' co-operative. A new company, Crown Winsor, took over after about eighteen months, producing their own and some SylvaC models but their operation was short-lived also and, despite the fact that someone else tried to resurrect part of the SylvaC interest, the factory closed and was sold in 1989. The present owners, Portmeirion, have indicated that they have no plans to use the SylvaC moulds, still in the factory, along with their own production.

People collect pottery for all sorts of reasons, but when a pottery company ceases to exist, their products become even more sought after. SylvaC is no exception and over the last few years it has become **extremely** sought after - and therefore, in some cases, quite high priced, with more and more collectors searching for fewer and fewer pieces. Fortunately, SylvaC was produced in fairly high quantities, so there is still a lot of pieces around, but it is not an endless supply! The majority of collectors go for the coloured matt glazed items but, in more recent years, **anything** SylvaC has become collectable. The majority, again, collect the animals and animal-related wares but the later-produced novelty kitchen wares (e.g. the Face Pots) have recently rocketed in popularity and price, some examples fetching well over £100! There are some collectors, of course, who collect the early ornate vases, jugs and jardinieres, others who collect only matt green pieces or matt fawn, or blue, those who collect just vases or jugs. Such was the incredible variety of pieces made by Shaw and Copestake that the list is endless and the opportunities for the collector abound. There is something for everyone.

9

THE SYLVAC COLLECTORS CIRCLE

In 1988, more in a quest for information and communication with other like-minded people, The SylvaC Collectors Circle was formed by Mick and Derry Collins. Mick and Derry, husband and wife collectors from Horndean in Hampshire, had started collecting SylvaC in the early 1980's when nothing much was known about its origins and history. It was at that time very cheap in price and, in the main, regarded as rubbish and not worth a second glance! (How things have changed!) They met other collectors also interested, so the idea of a club was born and realised in June 1988, the object being to gain more information and to convey that in turn to others who might be interested. Today, ten years later, The SylvaC Collectors Circle has around five hundred members, in the U.K. and overseas, with several new members joining each week. Mick and Derry both have full-time jobs but, in their spare time they run the club and produce four club newsletters a year, together with an extremely popular series of Information Sheets, containing coloured pictures, information and prices on selected SylvaC categories (Dogs, Lazy Pixies, Animals, Face Pots, etc., etc.). Information via the club is also freely available to club members and they are encouraged to keep in touch by either telephone or letter (or fax!) to tell of their finds, their experiences, their collections or anything SylvaC, in order to 'spread the word' through the eagerly awaited newsletter. Mick and Derry spend most of any time left (when the garden or decorating doesn't call!) visiting car boot sales, antiques fairs and fleamarkets to boost their own collection and to perhaps find pieces that other club members are looking for.

One of the aims of the club is, and always has been, to provide its members with as much information as they require, to enable them to buy wisely and avoid the many pitfalls that seem to accompany any form of collecting - and to make it enjoyable at the same time! As things are at present, careful selection of SylvaC pieces at reasonable prices can be a good investment for the future.

Currently the annual club membership fee is £15, U.K. members, and £20, overseas members. If you wish to join The SylvaC Collectors Circle, please send an S.A.E. for details. The address is:- SylvaC Collectors Circle, 174, Portsmouth Road, Horndean, Waterlooville, Hants. PO8 9HP. Telephone 01705 591725. (Fax: 01705 788494, E-mail: sylvac.club@mcmail.com, Web site: www.sylvac.mcmail.com).

RECOGNITION

Collecting SylvaC can be a bit of a minefield and mistakes can sometimes be costly. There are no hard and fast pointers to aid recognition but, perhaps, the following few tips may help avoid some of the pitfalls.

The most common misapprehension about SylvaC is that everything produced had the name stamped somewhere on it. This is definitely not true - remember, the name SylvaC was not devised until the mid-1930's and it was seldom used on the pottery itself until around 1945. It is also untrue that if a piece **originated** in the 1930's it will not have a name on it. These two statements may sound totally contradictory but there is an explanation. Take as an example the no.1378 Terrier, perhaps the best known of all the SylvaC dogs. This item was first produced circa 1938 and would not have had the SylvaC name on it, at that time. As the mould was used right up until 1982, the name was subsequently added to it and the later productions will have the name either impressed into the base or rubber-stamped under the glaze. This applies to many pieces that were first manufactured in the thirties and which continued in the post-war years and beyond. In a nutshell, models that were actually produced in the 1930's do not have the name on them. On post-1945 productions, and on some 1930's pieces that were continued throughout the 1940's, and up until the factory closed, it was usual, where the item had sufficient space on the underside, to impress the name or to rubber-stamp it somewhere. Still taking the 1378 Terrier as the example, if one is found with no name on it, but with the mould number on it (obviously), it is assumed to be pre-1945. There are, as you can well imagine, exceptions to the rule!

Early Shaw and Copestake items, the ornate vases, jugs, etc. are not, strictly speaking, SylvaC - that was the name given to the novelties, animals, etc. that began life in the early 1930's as cellulose pieces, and went on to be matt glazed and, later, bright glazed. Strictly speaking, again, these novelties, animals, etc. were not SylvaC when they were first made - they were named thus later! However, collectors everywhere now regard all of the products of Shaw and Copestake as SylvaC, the 1894-1930 pieces usually referred to as 'early SylvaC'. These early pieces generally have just the mould number on them, impressed in a particular style of numbering (illustrated overleaf) and, in the majority of cases, 'MADE IN ENGLAND', if space permits. A number of models also may have a registration number on them, and some may have what is termed the 'Daisy' backstamp, or mark.

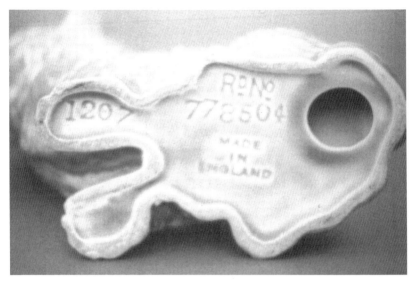

1930's piece with impressed mould number, registration number and origin.

The same 1930's piece, but with impressed mould number, registration number, origin **and** name. (Note the difference in mould shape).

1930's piece with impressed mould number, registration number applied for and origin (plus, price label for £18!).

1940's piece with impressed mould number, raised origin and potters mark. Faint rubber-stamped 'SylvaC'.

13

1940's piece with impressed mould number and origin. Rubber-stamped 'SylvaC' and faint potter's mark ('M')

1950's piece with impressed mould number, name, origin and size. Word 'SIZE' is in a different style (hand written). Faint raised potter's mark ('L') under mould number.

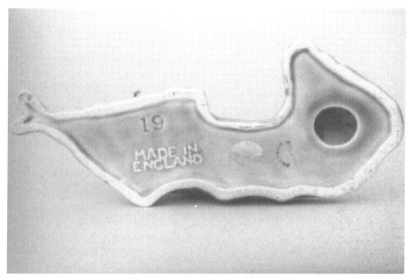

1950's piece with impressed Falcon factory number, raised origin and rubber-stamped 'SylvaC England'

1950's Falcon factory piece with raised mould number, potter's mark and 'Falcon' name, but with rubber stamped 'SylvaC Made in England'.

The mould number, origin (Made in England) and registration markings are usually much clearer on the productions of the early 1930's which were not glazed but finished in cellulose, a much thinner coating. Items, such as vases, plant pots, clocks, etc. may have an additional four figure number on them, usually in gold - this is the design number.

The mould numbering system, i.e. the number that was impressed into each piece, has, for collectors, proved to be very confusing. From the beginning Shaw and Copestake allocated sequential numbers to items they made and, until the late 1930's, everything was straightforward, with the numbers reaching the 1500 mark. Then in approximately 1940, due to the war, production of SylvaC was shifted to the Thomas Lawrence (Falcon Ware) factory and SylvaC which originated there was allocated new numbering - (horror of horrors for collectors) it started at number '1' again and had reached approximately number '760' when production ceased there in 1957. This, of course, resulted in there being two sets of numbers 1-760 (approx.). The Shaw and Copestake factory set covered the years 1900-1931 and the Thomas Lawrence factory set covered the years 1940-1957! Thus, after the war years, when the Shaw and Copestake factory was producing products again, they continued from 1500 whereas the Thomas Lawrence factory was using low three-figure numbers! To add to this complication some of the pieces made at the Thomas Lawrence factory had **raised** numbering and there are even pieces around with both the SylvaC **and** Falcon Ware marks on them! To sum up, a high proportion of SylvaC does have the mould number impressed on the base somewhere, in a particular style of lettering (see pages 12 to 14) but there are other pieces that have raised numbers and some on which there is no visible evidence of name or number.

SYLVAC 'LOOKALIKES'

It would seem that when a pottery produced a good idea and had an item that was popular, some other pottery would copy it! This appears to have happened with a number of items which has now resulted in many SylvaC collectors, particularly the newer ones, having great difficulty recognising the **genuine** SylvaC items. This is made even more difficult by traders who mark obviously non-SylvaC pieces with a label stating that the item is SylvaC. For more experienced collectors this is not usually a problem but it does take time to become familiar with SylvaC products and finishes. It is therefore easy to make mistakes when first starting out on the 'SylvaC trail' and over a number of years it has become clear that certain items turn up again and again which bring forth the question - could this be SylvaC? Well-known matt glazed 'lookalikes', as they are known, include many snub-nose rabbits, with no markings on them, or with the numbers '0', '1', '304', ..., etc., dogs which look like the no.1378, 1379 and 1380 Terrier but which have no markings at all, a similar dog with the name 'Roddy Ware' on it, a number of dogs numbered 34 to 38 and which sometimes have the name H.A. Wain (Melba Ware) on them, a squirrel eating an acorn, sometimes with the number 539 on it and a small bear wearing short trousers and braces, sometimes with the number 538 on it. Other frequently mistaken items are, a black cellulose 'British Bulldog', sitting, (sometimes with beads for eyes - SylvaC **never** used beads as eyes!), with no base markings, poor quality lop-ear rabbits, with no base markings, and a trio of different height dogs joined together and sometimes numbered 717. None of these pieces are SylvaC productions, although they may be seen labelled as such. There are, of course, other examples, but these mentioned here are by far the most queried. Quite honestly, if some of the pieces above are put alongside genuine pieces of SylvaC, the difference is very, very obvious. Not so easy though, when a item is seen on its own in a pile of junk on a car boot stall!

Since the Sylvan Works closed altogether in 1989, prior to its new lease of life under its present owners, there has been another, and more serious, problem for SylvaC collectors, particularly new collectors. At the time of closure, there were literally hundreds of unfinished pieces within the factory, mostly in the 'biscuit' stage. (That is the stage where the pottery has been fired and is waiting to be decorated and glazed). Many of these pieces have been decorated and glazed **since**, mostly very badly and not to the original SylvaC specification. A number of dogs, for example, have been seen around the car boot sales and fairs, etc. in a basic shiny fawn glaze (if 'glaze' is the right word!) with none of the usual decoration for the highlights, such as eyes, noses, etc. Some have even been seen with the eyes painted **on top** of the glaze. A few collectors have been quite adamant that these pieces they've bought are genuine SylvaC - because they've got the name on them - not so! There are moulds, too, that have been sold to other potteries that still have the SylvaC number on them but are now in totally different finishes to the SylvaC original. Good examples of original SylvaC moulds turning up in new guises are the 1086 and 1087 Cats. These first started re-appearing a while ago in bright glaze white, decorated all over with flowers! Another mould, not

SylvaC was made in order that a smaller cat could be included, that matched the other two, and it was given the number 1085. A complete set of these now three cats, with 'bad crazing', has even been seen at an antique fair and they were labelled 'early SylvaC cats' and were priced at over £100! With the demand for SylvaC as it is, who knows what might happen next, in order to fox the eager collector.

FINISHES

Four types of finish, basically, were used on Shaw and Copestake products. These were:-

Hand Decorated/Gilded

The description of the finish applied to the early Shaw and Copestake products of the 1900's to the late 1920's. A base colour was given to the pottery and decoration of patterns, scenes, etc. was either hand done or applied by transfer. Many items had gold decoration on them, giving them a more expensive look. Vases and pots can still be found nowadays with the gold decoration in excellent condition. As mentioned earlier, many of these items have a four-figure design number in gold on them.

Cellulose

This was a paint finish used, in the main, from the late 1920's through to the early 1940's. There were some odd items that were cellulosed after this, including the garden-type Gnomes. Visually, cellulosed SylvaC bears a resemblance to the old plaster figures - it is just literally painted pottery. In some cases the models were painted with several colours, but in others a single colour (black, orange, cream/brown, etc.) was used. The finish was not very durable, subject to fading and flaking (and being touched up!) but good examples still exist. Many of the popular lines of the matt glaze and bright glaze eras were originally cellulosed.

Matt Glaze

By far the most collectable of all SylvaC, the coloured matt glazes were introduced in the early 1930's and continued (albeit in limited quantities) right up until 1982 when all production ceased. The finish is slightly shiny but has more of a satin look and it was available in several colours. The fawn was probably the most popular and this was the colour that survived the longest, followed by green and blue. The darker green and blues are generally the earlier pieces but the blue finish was comparatively short-lived and is now considered quite rare. Other colours used included brown, cream, ivory, pink and, later, turquoise and yellow. There were also mixtures of colours, giving unusual effects on jugs, vases, bowls, etc. The M101 finish, a mixture of fawn, green and cream, was probably the most widely used of the 'mixtures'.

Bright Glaze
This is the shiny or gloss finish used from the late 1940's until production ceased altogether. Many of the earlier plain, single colour matt pieces, particularly the animals, were finished in bright glaze over a hand decorated base, giving them a very lifelike appearance.

It must be borne in mind that SylvaC was never intended to be a high grade product and therefore the finished object was often subject to glazing faults and other imperfections. Matt glaze pieces often had patches of the colour and glaze missing, particularly on the pointed parts of a model. On the later bright glaze items (although it occurs on matt items to a lesser degree) there is much evidence to be seen now of crazing, the appearance of fine cracks in the glaze, but unless the cracks actually go right through the pottery, this shouldn't be seen as a problem. Chips should be regarded as damage - the items were not originally chipped, but any under-glaze chip is acceptable. As a collector purchasing SylvaC, care should also be taken inspecting the piece for damage, bad restoration, attempted repair, etc. A restored or repaired piece should have a note to that effect on its label and be priced accordingly. This is often not the case and, unless you spot damage or restoration, you may not be told! Talking of labels, some items may have the original factory label still stuck on them - others may have had labels added to them since, to encourage a sale!

RARITY AND VALUE

As with all other areas of collecting there are pieces which are very, very common and others which are extremely rare. Again, SylvaC is no exception to this. Certain items which are listed in SylvaC publications are seen monotonously over and over again, whereas other items have never been seen and may, in fact, never have actually made it to the production line. They were just a modeller's sample, an idea or prototype, entered in the factory Mould Makers Register, but not ever mass-produced. Then there are, of course, pieces that turn up, of which there is no known record. These pieces are referred to as 'unlisteds' or 'No information', in publications. In these instances, if the item is an animal or novelty piece the price would normally reflect its rarity. Conversely, the more common pieces should be at the lower end of the price scale. However, this is where difficulty creeps in, particularly for new collectors. What is common or rare, if the piece is being seen for the first time? The Information Sheets and newsletters of the S.C.C. can be a useful guide and thus help avoid costly mistakes when buying something, stated as being rare, when it is not. 'Rare' pieces frequently aren't! It's just that the person selling hasn't seen it before! Or, maybe the buyer hasn't. The S.C.C. gives, in its publications, a 'rarity guide' which indicates the chances (or not!) of seeing a particular item. Although not completely infallible, it's better than no guide at all! Items are divided into four categories, namely [R] for rarely seen, [FR] for fairly rarely seen, [FF] for fairly frequently seen and [F] for very frequently seen, or common.

It is not **only** rarity, or availability, that decides the value of a piece. Other factors determine this, such as finish, colour, size, condition and age. It is not possible to give hard and fast guidelines when it comes to what one should pay for a particular item because, in the end, that decision is for the buyer to make. There are still many items around that can be bought for under £20 but certain categories automatically command higher prices, due to the high demand for them, e.g. animals and household novelties (the 'Face Pots'). The matt glazed items are probably the most sought after and become more expensive in the more unusual colours of blue, dark brown, pink, etc. Cellulosed and bright glazed pieces, unless very rare, are generally less expensive than matt glaze but, again, if they are animal/animal-related they are going to be more expensive than vases, jardinieres, bowls, etc.

20

LOCATING SYLVAC

Collectors often ask, 'Where's the best place to find SylvaC?'. The answer is, virtually anywhere where somebody is selling something secondhand! For the new collector just starting out, probably the best hunting grounds are the antique fairs. Large or small, very few fairs have no SylvaC whatsoever and it does not always follow that the larger the fair, the more SylvaC there is. Nor does it follow that the larger the fair, the higher the price charged for it. Many reasonably priced pieces have been found at the larger fairs, although there are always exceptions. Some small fairs may have just the piece you're looking for and, in any case, stock changes regularly. There are also many antiques centres and shops around the country where there are some good finds awaiting the collector. Even up-market antique shops have yielded some interesting pieces, too. Charity and bric-a-brac shops have produced some exciting finds from time to time, as have fleamarkets and car boot sales, where some rarer items have been found. Church fairs, bazaars, fetes and charity auctions are also possibilities. Auctions, at one time, rarely produced any SylvaC at all but nowadays a lot of it goes to auction and, in some cases, goes through the roof! Beware though, there have been many instances where repaired or restored SylvaC has been channelled through auction rooms and, of late, post-SylvaC pieces are finding their way into some auctions, as a means of 'dumping' them - post-SylvaC items are original SylvaC moulds, decorated and finished by persons unknown, after the factory closed down. As mentioned earlier, they are usually badly finished and lacking the original SylvaC detail - in the case of dogs - no highlighted eyes, noses, etc. and the finish may well be in colours never used on the originals. Very recently, some reproductions are beginning to appear, e.g. The no.1960 Stork Handle Jug, slightly smaller than the original and in a slightly brighter green. Any item manufactured or finished after 1982, when Shaw and Copestake ceased trading, is not generally regarded as genuine SylvaC nor is an original SylvaC mould bearing another company's name.

At **any** of the above events, or locations, is the possibility of finding a piece of SylvaC but it is by no means a certainty. Many collectors go from one to the other regularly and in different areas of the country, in their search for an elusive piece, or a bargain. A place said to be good on one occasion may not be on the next and vice versa. The idea is to keep at it and, above all, don't get despondent when nothing materialises for a while. The fun is in the chase (as they say) and, if it's a family thing, so much the better. Many a SylvaC collector now, started off as a spotter for their parents! Good luck!

Shaw & Copestake Pottery and SylvaC Ware

The following pictures illustrate the products of Shaw and Copestake, in date order, together with details of mould numbers, decade (or year) in which they were **first** produced, the finish illustrated and their 1998 values. The pictures give an indication of the vast range of products, manufactured from the 1900's to the 1970's and to their diversity.

1900's no.75 Vase, with various designs. Transfer printed with hand decorated overlay gilding. Value: £25-£30 each. (This vase shape was used until the late 1920's).

1900's no.127 Jardiniere with Roses design. Transfer printed with hand decorated overlay gilding. Value: £45-£55.

22

1900's no.183 Jardiniere. Transfer printed. Value: £25-£30.

1900's no.230 Clock. Transfer printed with hand decorated overlay gilding. Value: £65-£85.

1900's no.354 'Holborn' Vase and Stand. Transfer printed with hand decorated overlay gilding. Value: £200-£275 the pair.

1920's no.419 Vase. Transfer printed with hand decorated overlay gilding. Moonlight Ware design. Value: £50-£70 the pair. (A **pair** of vases has mirrored or complimentary scenes).

1920's no.540 Vase. Transfer printed with hand decorated overlay gilding. 'Swans' design. Scene on each vase slightly different, nevertheless they are a pair. Value: £50-£60.

1920's no.573 (size 5) Jug. Transfer printed. The basic jug was
decorated with many different designs but this is 'The Haven'
(design number unknown). Value: £20-£25.

1920's no.600 Vase with hunting scenes. Transfer printed with hand decorated overlay
gilding. Value: £40-£50 the pair.

1920's no.610 Vase. Cellulose finish. One pair Dutch design, single with yacht design. Value: £35-£45 pair, £20-£25 single.

1920's no.694 Clock Set. Lord and Lady design. Cellulose finish. Each piece numbered 694. Value: £60-£70 complete

Early 1930's no.700 Kingfisher. Cellulose finish. Value: £20-£30. Often with no.436 Bowl.

Early 1930's no.743 Airedale. Cellulose finish. Value: £65-£80. Believed to be the first 'SylvaC' dog.

Early 1930's no.788 Elephant with Howdah. Cellulose finish. Value: £25-£35. One of five different sizes.

Early 1930's no.793 Swan (Holder). Cellulose finish. Value: £30-£40. One of three different sizes.

Early 1930's no.819 Lion on no.822 Plinth. Matt glaze. Value: £160-£250. Example shown was manufactured as a lamp base.

Early 1930's no.917 Jug. Cellulose finish. Value: £20-£25.

Early 1930's no.920 Lady. Cellulose finish. Value: £95-£120.

Early 1930's (c.1933) no.1026, no.1027 and no.1028 Snub Nose Rabbit, or Bunny. Matt glaze. Value: £80-£100, £100-£150 and £150-£200. Eight sizes were produced - the smallest, no.1400 is shown to compare size - the others are nos.1065, 990, 1067, and 1386.

c.1933 no.1038 Dog. Cellulose finish. Value: £30-£45. The smallest of four sizes - others are nos. 1043, 1044 and 1045.

c.1934 no.1115 Squirrel and Acorn Flower Jug. Matt glaze. Value: £40-£55. Was also made in a version with a spout (no.1959), a miniature (no.1993) and a bright glaze model (no.4068).

29

c.1936 nos.1205-1209 Mac Dog, (size 1, the smallest, is 1205). Matt glaze. Value: £25-£35 (1205), £45-£60 (1206), £65-£70 (1207), £75-£95 (1208) and £140-£160 (1209).

c.1936 no.1226 Clown Wall Plaque. Matt glaze. Value: £120-£150.

c.1937 no.1366 Ashtray. Matt glaze. Value: £30-£45. Same basic shape ashtray may be seen with different animals. Ashtray and animals are in contrasting colours.

c.1937 no.1373 Kid. Matt glaze. Value: £45-£55.

c.1937 no.1377 Pigeon. Matt glaze. Value: £75-£95.

31

c.1937 no.1378, no.1379 and no.1380 Terrier. Matt glaze. Value: £25-£35, £45-£65 and £120-£150.

c.1937 no.1388 Hare, crouching, size 2. Matt glaze. Value: £120-£140. One of three different sizes - others are no.1371 and 1389.

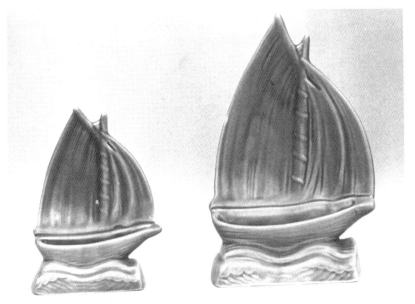

c.1938 no.1393 Yacht Posy Holder, size 1 and no.1394 Yacht Posy Holder, size 2. Matt glaze. Value: £25-£30, £30-£40. Size 3 is no.1340.

continued on page 41

COLOUR SECTION

Shaw and Copestake Vases.

No.	363	606	614	no number
Value	£20-£30	£35-£45	£25-£35	£15-£25

Early Cellulose Animals.

843	846	1144	1159
Laughing Cat	Panther with Howdah	Squirrel with Acorn	Corkscrew Cat
£45-£65	£50-£85	£30-£45	£65-£95

Early Cellulose Novelties

962	1081	1222	1288
Gnome, standing	Red Riding Hood	Billikin	Welsh Lady
£80-£95	£80-£95	£60-£75	£25-£35

Matt Glaze Dogs

1191	2584	3096	3126	3827
'Joey' Dog	Howling Dog	Dog, sitting	Dog, lying	Spaniel with Slipper
£50-£75	£65-£85	£45-£60	£45-£60	£55-£75

Matt Glaze Animals

1333	1374	1518	1659	2980
Cat, crouching	Donkey	Squirrel eating Nut	Lamb	'Bugs Bunny'
£85-£110	£55-£75	£45-£60	£40-£55	£65-£85

Matt Glaze Novelty Posy Holders

586	1996	2054	2660
Dog in Barrel	Dog with Basket	Scottie with Basket	Urn with City Dog
£25-£35	£25-£35	£25-£35	£25-£35

35

Matt Glaze Novelty Ashtrays

1454	1455	1622	1573
With 1522 Bear Cub	With 1432 Cat	Fireplace	Armchair
£25-£35	£25-£35	£20-£30	£20-£30

Matt Glaze Bookends

1311	1311	1546	1546
with 1259 Dog	with 1386 Rabbit	with 1509 Rabbit	with 1512 Dog
£35-£45	£35-£45	£35-£45	£40-£50

Matt Glaze Jardinieres/Bowls

409	1783	3015
Jardiniere	Bowl - Dahlia	Jardiniere - Oakwood
£25-£35	£15-£25	£15-£25

Honey/Jam Pots

585	1849	2046	2105
Strawberry	Dogs Head	Ivy Leaf	Chrys
Bright glaze	Matt glaze	Matt glaze	Matt glaze
£20-£30	£35-£50	£25-£35	£25-£35

Bright Glaze Novelty Tankards

4720	4721	4725	4727
Cricket Ball	Football	Bowls	Fishing
£25-£35	£25-£35	£25-£35	£25-£35

Novelty Jugs

43	305	398	561	4744
Duck	Cavalier	Rose Bud	Jug	Maple Leaf
Matt glaze	Matt glaze	Bright glaze	Matt glaze	Bright glaze
£45-£60	£20-£30	£20-£30	£20-£30	£20-£30

Character Jugs

no number	1463	2892	5114
Henry Vlll	Neville Chamberlain	Abraham Lincoln	Robin Hood
Matt glaze	Cellulose	Bright glaze	Bright glaze
£30-£45	£70-£85	£55-£75	£45-£60

Bright Glaze Dogs

3078	3275	3314	3321	3933
Dachshund,	Spaniel,	Smooth Haired	Alsatian,	Pomeranian,
sitting	with Pipe	Fox Terrier	sitting	sitting
£30-£45	£40-£50	£30-£45	£25-£35	£40-£50

Bright Glaze Money Boxes

5096	5097	5659	5662
Bulldog	Frog	Elephant	Fish
£25-£30	£25-£30	£35-£45	£35-£50

Bright Glaze Animals

92	98	99	3150
Baby Elephant	Chimp	Siamese Cat	Foal
£30-£40	£30-£40	£25-£35	£25-£35

continued from page 32

c.1938 no.1400. Matt glaze. Value: £25-£50 (some are much rarer than others). The number 1400 was allocated c.1938 to miniature animals, although some of the above were produced much later. A few of the items had their own individual number also, e.g. the mouse is no.106 and the duck is no.3115.

c.1938 no.1413 Triple Rustic Fence Posy Holder. Matt glaze. Value: £20-£30.

c.1938 no.1428 Donkey. Matt glaze. Value: £35-£40.

c.1939 no.1492 Duck, size 3. Matt glaze. Value: £90-£120. Largest of three - others are nos.1498 and 1499.

c.1939 no.1478 Twin Posy/Spill Holder with Cat. Matt glaze. Value: £25-£35.

c.1940 no.1500 Panda. Cellulose finish. Value: £45-£55. Very few items were cellulosed after the 1940's. A similar Panda is no.1506.

c.1944 no.1748 Dish from the Neptune range. Bright glaze. Value: £30-£40.

Late 1940's (c.1948) no.1851 Basket from the Wild Duck range. Matt glaze. Value: £20-£25.

Late 1940's (c.1949) no.1868 Bowl with Lid from the Blackberry range. Bright glaze. Value: £18-£25.

The pieces shown on this and the following two pages are Falcon Ware factory pieces - hence the low numbers again.

Late 1940's/early 1950's no.15 Horse, standing. Bright glaze. Value: £45-£60.

Late 1940's/early 1950's no.18 Spaniel, sitting. Matt glaze. Value: £35-£45.

Late 1940's/early 1950's no.88 Spaniel Head Wall Plaque. Bright glaze. Value: £35-£40.

1950's no.136 Tortoise Trinket Box. Matt glaze. Value: £120-£150.

1950's no.166 Sealyhams Joined. Matt glaze. Value: £60-£80.

1950's no.183 Comical Mule and no.184 Boxing Cat. Matt glaze. Value: £60-£70, £55-£65. No.3141 Boxing Monkey completes this trio.

1950's no.349 Handbag Vase. Matt glaze.
Value: £65-£85.

1950's no.475 Miniature Stork Jug.
Matt glaze. Value: £15-£20.

1950's no.544 Jug and no.545 Basket from the Budgie range. Matt glaze. Value: £65-£85, £55-£65.

1949 no number Commemorative Plate   and the reverse side details.
Matt glaze. Value: £25-£30.

1950's no.1934 (size 3), no.1910 (size 1) and no.1933 (size 2) Sweets dishes. Bright glaze.
Value: £25-£30 (size 3), £15-£20 (size 1) and £20-£25 (size 2).

48

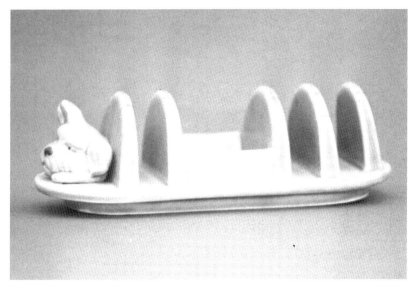

1950's no.1990 Toast Rack from the Dog's Head range. Matt glaze. Value: £45-£55.

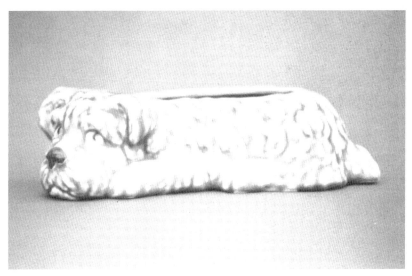

1950's no.2024 Sealyham Posy Holder. Matt glaze. Value: £20-£25.

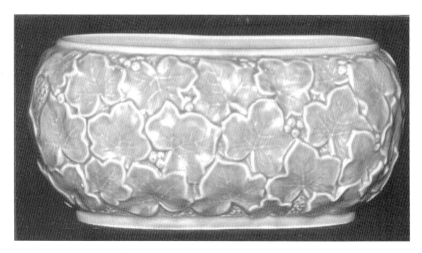

1950's no.2035 Bowl from the Ivy Leaf range. Matt glaze. Value: £20-£25.

1950's no.2062 Bulb Bowl with Scottie Dogs (in use!). Matt finish. Value: £40-£45.

1950's no.2093 Miniature Jug, no.2095 Jug and no.2118 Vase from the Chrys range. Matt glaze. Value: £15-£25, £30-£35 and £25-£30.

1950's no.2158 Candle Holder - upturned mushroom and gnome. Matt glaze. Value: £45-£60.

1950's no.2178 Posy Trough, no.2189 Miniature Vase and no.2213 Jardiniere from the Raphique range. Bright glaze and matt glaze. Value: £12-£15, £5-£8 and £20-£25.

1950's no.2228 Plant Pot with swirls pattern. Matt glaze. Value: £15-£25.

1950's no.2249 Jardiniere and no.2252 Vase from the Cactus range. Matt glaze. Value: £15-£20 and £20-£25.

1950's no.2339 Bulb Bowl with Lazy Pixie. Matt glaze. Value: £40-£50.

1950's no.2425 Chimney Posy Holder with various figures. Matt glaze. Value: £25-£30.

1950's no.2451 (size 4) and no.2455 (size 3) Toothache Dog. Matt glaze. Other two sizes are 3093 (size 1) and 3183 (size 2). Value: £200-£250 and £110-£140.

1960's no.2537 Greyhound. Bright glaze. Value:£25-£35.

1960's no.2626 Vase and no.2683 Posy Holder from the Moselle range. Matt glaze. Value: £20-£30 and £15-£20.

1960's no.2706 Vase and no.2710 Jardiniere from the Jewel range. Matt glaze. Value: £20-£25, £15-£20.

1960's no.2743 Posy Vase from the Bamboo range. Matt glaze. Value: £20-£25.

1960's no.2795 Flat Cat (size 3). Bright glaze. Value: £65-£85.

1960's no.2829 Pen Holder with 'Pam' figure. Bright glaze. Value: £50-£75.

1960's no.2841 Shakespeare Book Holder. Bright glaze. Value: £35-£40.

1960's no.2874 Jardiniere from the Apple Blossom range. Matt glaze. Value: £25-£30.

1960's no.2899 'John F. Kennedy' Character Jug. Bright glaze. Value: £55-£75.

1960's no.2938 (size 1), no.2950 (size 2) and no.2951 (size 3) 'Hang Dogs'. Matt glaze.
Value: £15-£18, £20-£25 and £30-£35.

1960's no.2993 Jardiniere from the Magnolia range. Matt glaze. Value: £25-£30.

1960's no.3011 Vase from the Wyka range. Matt glaze. Value: £20-£25.

These two included in a batch of mould numbers issued to the Falcon works in the 1950's.

1950's no.3151 Cat. Matt glaze. Value: £30-£40.

1950's no.3123 Comical Dog. Matt glaze.
Value: £55-£70.

1960's no.3285 Jardiniere and no.3289 Posy Trough from the Lily range. Matt glaze. Value:
£65-£85 and £25-£35.

1960's no.3370 Seahorse Bowl. Matt glaze.
Value: £25-£35.

1960's no.3542 Mr. SylvaC Ashtray. Bright
glaze. Original had the words, 'For Quality
& Value' on the front edge of the base. The
example shown is a 1980's re-issue. Value:
£100-£150.

1960's no.3710 Jardiniere, no.3722 Plant Pot and no.3725 Vase from the Palm Leaf range.
Matt glaze. Value: £18-£25, £20-£25 and £15-£20.

1960's no.3930 Bull from the Prestige range of animals. Bright glaze. Value: £80-£120.

1960's no.4233 Vase from the Woodland range and no.4394 Bowl from the Riverside range. Bright glaze. Value: £15-£20 and £20-£25.

1970's no.4750 Coleslaw (top), no.4752 Piccalilli, no.4753 Chutney and no.4754 Parsley Face Pots. Bright glaze. Values: £60-£90, £60-£90, £30-£40 and £75-£100.

1970's no.4871 Leaf Honey Base with 4867 Raspberry Lid. Bright glaze. Value: £25-£30.

1970's no.4896 Orange Face Pot. Bright glaze. Value: £50-£85.

Please note that during the 1970's some numbers were used out of sequence.

1970's no.4966 Bath Salts Holder from the Mosaic range. Bright glaze. Value: £30-£40.

1970's no.4988 West Highland Terrier from the Supreme Dogs range. Bright glaze. Value: £25-£35

1970's no.5006 and no.5010 Plant Pots from the Churnet range. Matt glaze. Value: £15-£20, £20-£30.

63

1970's no.5038 Tea Bag Holder. Bright glaze.
Value: £20-£25.

1970's no.5048 Horseradish Face Pot.
Bright glaze. Value: £75-£140.

1970's no.5106 Owl Money Box. Bright
glaze. Value: £20-£25.

1980's no.5661 Bassett Hound Money Box.
Matt glaze. Value: £30-£40.

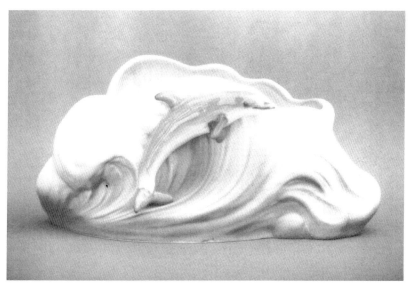

1970's no.5185 Bowl from the Dolphin range. Matt glaze. Value: £25-£30.

1970's no.5209 Fox from the Prestige range of animals. Bright glaze. Value: £50-£85.

1970's no.5248 Posy Basket from the Harvest Time range. Matt glaze. Value: £15-£20.

1970's no.5260 Whippet from the Supreme Dogs range. Bright glaze. Value: £25-£30.

1970's no.5295, no.5296 and no.5297 Novelty Dogs. Matt glaze. Value: £25-£35 (size 3), £20-£25 (size 2) and £15-£20 (size 1).

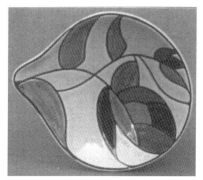

1970's no.5386 Dish from the Lincoln range. Bright glaze. Value: £15-£20.

1970's no.5343 Cruet from the Cordon Brun range. Matt glaze. Value £15-£20.

1980 no.5423 Teatime Set. Clock on the beaker shows 3 o'clock. Bright glaze. Value: £25-£30.

1970's no.5460 Bell from the Anniversary range. Bright glaze. Value: £15-£20. This example commemorating the 1981 marriage of Charles and Diana.

1970's no.5521 Spaniel Pendant. Bright glaze. Value: £35-£45. Strictly speaking the number is 5521/1 as 5521 was the brooch version.

1970's no.5997 Matchbox Holder, no.6001 Gift Parcel Box, no.6002 Carrier Bag Holder and no.6003 Parcel Money Box from the Desk Top range. Matt glaze. Values: £25-£30, £25-£30, £15-£20 and £15-£20.

INDEX TO MOULD NUMBERS

No.	Page	No.	Page	No.	Page	No.	Page
15	45	788	27	1400	41	2228	52
18	45	793	27	1413	41	2249	53
43	38	819	28	1428	42	2252	53
75	22	843	33	1454	36	2339	53
88	45	846	33	1455	36	2425	54
92	40	917	28	1463	39	2451	54
98	40	920	28	1478	42	2455	54
99	40	962	34	1492	42	2537	55
127	22	1026	29	1500	43	2584	34
136	45	1027	29	1518	35	2626	55
166	46	1028	29	1546	36	2660	35
183	23	1038	29	1573	36	2683	55
183	46	1081	34	1622	36	2706	56
184	46	1115	29	1659	35	2710	56
230	23	1144	33	1748	43	2743	56
305	38	1159	33	1783	37	2795	56
349	47	1191	34	1849	37	2829	57
354	23	1205	30	1851	44	2841	57
363	33	1206	30	1868	44	2874	57
398	38	1207	30	1910	48	2892	39
409	37	1208	30	1933	48	2899	57
419	24	1209	30	1934	48	2938	58
475	47	1222	34	1990	49	2950	58
540	24	1226	30	1996	35	2951	58
544	47	1288	34	2024	49	2980	35
545	47	1311	36	2035	50	2993	58
561	38	1333	35	2046	37	3011	58
573	25	1366	31	2054	35	3015	37
585	37	1373	31	2062	50	3078	39
586	35	1374	35	2093	51	3096	34
600	25	1377	31	2095	51	3123	59
606	33	1378	32	2105	37	3126	34
610	26	1379	32	2118	51	3150	40
614	33	1380	32	2158	51	3151	59
694	26	1388	32	2178	52	3275	39
700	27	1393	32	2189	52	3285	59
743	27	1394	32	2213	52	3289	59

No.	Page	No.	Page	No.	Page	No.	Page
3314	39	4725	38	5038	64	5386	67
3321	39	4727	38	5048	64	5423	67
3370	60	4744	38	5096	40	5460	68
3542	60	4750	62	5097	40	5521	68
3710	60	4752	62	5106	64	5659	40
3722	60	4753	62	5114	39	5661	64
3725	60	4754	62	5185	65	5662	40
3827	34	4867	62	5209	65	5997	68
3930	61	4871	62	5248	66	6001	68
3933	39	4896	62	5260	66	6002	68
4233	61	4966	63	5295	66	6003	68
4394	61	4988	63	5296	66		
4720	38	5006	63	5297	66		
4721	38	5010	63	5343	67		

Cover Details

Front Cover: Top, L. to R. 1930's no.1504 Dog with paw in Basket. Matt glaze. Value: £55-£75. 1950's no.2209 Bowl from the Cactus range. Matt glaze. Value: £15-£25. 1930's no.1378 Terrier. Matt glaze. Value: £40-£50.
Bottom, L. to R. 1930's no.1067 Snub Nose Rabbit. Matt glaze. Value: £65-£85. 1930's no.1421 Lucky Pixie. Matt glaze. Value: £30-£40. 1930's no.1303 Lop Ear Rabbit. Matt glaze. Value: £180-£250. 1930's no.3115 Miniature Duckling. Matt glaze. Value: £35-£45. (This is numbered 1400 in some sales literature). 1930's no.1022 Boy with banjo. Cellulose finish. Value: £95-£130.

Back Cover: Top, L. to R. 1930's no.1451 Stag. Bright glaze. Value: £35-£40. 1970's no.4752 Piccalilli Face Pot. Bright glaze. Value: £60-£90. 1950's no.99 Siamese Cat. Bright glaze. Value: £25-£35. 1950's no.130 Penguin. Bright glaze. Value: £45-£65. 1950's no.398 Rose Bud Jug. Bright glaze. Value: £20-£30. 1970's no.4490 Life Guard Character Jug. Bright glaze. Value: £35-£45.

S ⅃ Ɔ PUBLICATIONS

The following publications may be obtained from The SylvaC Collectors Circle:-

THE SYLVAC STORY by Susan Jean Verbeek. Price £16.95, plus £2.00 p. & p.

THE SYLVAC COMPANION by Susan Jean Verbeek. Price £16.95, plus £2.00 p. & p.

THE SYLVAC COLLECTORS HANDBOOK - PART 1 - Second Edition by Anthony Van Der Woerd. Price £8.50, plus £1.00 p & p.

THE SYLVAC COLLECTORS HANDBOOK - PART 2 by Anthony Van Der Woerd. Price £8.50, plus £1.00 p. & p.

THE FALCON WARE STORY - by Susan Jean Verbeek. Price £17.95, plus £2.00 p. & p..

INFORMATION SHEETS by SCC. Price £3.00 each, inc. p. & p. Available exclusively to club members.

1.	Big 'Ead Dogs	11.	Novelty Ash Trays
2.	The Lazy Pixies	12.	Animals - 1
3.	Rabbits	13.	Horses
4.	Face Pots - 1	14.	Novelty Posy Holders
5.	Flower Pots	15.	Cats
6.	Jugs	16.	Dogs - 2
7.	Face Pots - 2	17.	Jugs - 2 (Miniatures)
8.	Bears and Pandas	18.	Dogs - 3
9.	Dogs - 1	19.	Animals - 2
10.	Figures	20.	Money Boxes

Each of the INFORMATION SHEETS consists of coloured illustrations, rarity guide, information and price guide.

Further titles may be added from time to time - please check for details.

Cheque should be made payable to The SylvaC Collectors Circle.